INTRODUCTION
Human Brain :
The Thoughts & Emotions

The human race is blessed with a brain which distinguishes it from the rest of the animal world. The volume of human brain is the largest in proportion to its total body. In the course of evolution of life the volume of human brain increased from about 800cc to 1100cc. That part which was added to this brain material was what is now known as the frontal lobe. While the lower animals like apes have sloping forehead, the humans have a vertical shape in the front part of their head. In this part of the head, that the function of language, thinking & emotions are contained. While the rear part of the head, contains that part of the brain which conducts in-volunteer activities of men. The frontal part performs those functions which have established men as a superior species. One of the greatest gifts of nature to humans is the gift of language. It is only humans who have the benefit of articulate language. It is through this gift that the humans have progressed to the present dominant status. Firstly, language enables the achievements attained by one generation to be passed on to next generations. Language contains the record of the progress made by various generations. This is passed on to the succeeding generations through education which normally occupies almost one-forth of the total lives of human beings. Equipped by the vast store of the past knowledge, generations after generation proceed to advanced human progress. The internet is an example of such gradual progression of the race of humans. Language functions not only as storage of knowledge but also enables communication among individual. It is noteworthy that no other race of the animal kingdom possesses this quality of having a language the rest of the species including our nearest relatives the chimpanzees do not have the benefit of a language.

All the tender thoughts of man are recorded through its language in the form of manuals, novels and poetry. Successive generations pickup from the past attainments and further add their own contributions.

The Emotional Side of
Human Beings

R. K. Agnihotri

Indra Publishing House
www.indrapublishing.com

Published by:

Indra Publishing House

E-5/21, Arera Colony,
Habibganj Police Station Road,
Bhopal 462016
Phone: +91 755 4059620, 4030921
Telefax : +91 755 4030921
Email : manish@indrapublishing.com
　　　pramod@indrapublishing.com
Web. : www.indrapublishing.com
Copyright © 2013 R. K. Aghniotri
All Rights Reserved
Title : The Emotional Side of Human Being
Author : R. K. Aghniotri
Text Design & Cover Design: Pramod & Creative Team
First Print : 2014
ISBN : 978-93-82518-68-6
₹ : 70/-

Printed & published by Mr. Manish Gupta for Indra Publishing House, E-5/21, Arera Colony, Habibganj Police Station Road, Bhopal 462016 INDIA

Contents

1. Emotions shared by Human beings with other members of Animal Kingdom.   09

2. The incidents of the killing of a dove & Reaction of the mother.   15

3. The world of Literature – Record of Tender Human feelings.   20

4. The Evolutionary Value of Faith   22

5. The Faith in Action.   36

6. The Psychic Factors Affecting Human Nature   42

7. Mahatma Gandhi and his Faith: 56

8. Focused and unfocused Faiths   61

9. Different Objects of Faith   66

10. Hitler's Misplaced Faith in Aryan Superiority   69

11. Faith in 'God-Men'   72

12. Appendix Hindu Wisdom   77

Emotions Shared By Human Beings With Other Members Of Animal Kingdom

Human beings are at the pinnacle of the animal kingdom. While they share their physical features with the rest of the members of the animal world, they are special in possessing emotions of humane nature. There is a Sanskrit verse embody this thought.

आहार निद्रा भयं मैथुनम् च ।

During the course of their evolution man gained extraordinary strength because of the development of the human brain. Memory and communication through language, inheriting the knowledge acquired by earlier generations, reading and writing have been the development of man as the superior most product of evolution.

Tender feelings like pity and compassion have been special epithets of humans. The word humanity is used to describe the emotional site of man.

Here we may take stock of the steps through which human beings attend their present's position of the most successful species like other animals; man was also a tree-dweller. In the course of evolution man descended from trees, where he acquired an erect posture. Instead of using all the four limbs (the legs), he used only two legs for walking due to his erect posture, the other two upper limbs were thus released from the function of locomotion. In due course of evolution spinning millions of years these two upper limbs converted themselves into hands. Man acquired further efficiency when his thumbs became opposable to the fingers by the use of his thumb along with the other four fingers, man could hold tools further when he developed binocular vision. Instead of seeing of two sights separately with one eye either i.e. either on the left or on the right he could see things in front by using both the eyes. These binocular visions enabled him to judge distances and see the surroundings in an effective way. The forehead man greave into a vertical shape and the cranial capacity increased up to 1100 cubic centimeters. That part of the human brain which was accommodated in the frontal portion of the skull became the thinking and memory support of revolving man. The real portion of the brain continued to take care of the biological functions of the human body while the front part get developed to enable man to acquire superiority over the animal kingdom. One of the greatest achievements of this part of the brain was that man developed articulate communication.

Man started using language due to the development of his brain capacity. He could communicate with the help of this language with other fellow beings but the most important result of acquiring this capacity was that he could gain from the knowledge and experience acquired innumerable previous generations. The knowledge of the entire human development became ensconced in the books written in different languages. He could master the skills and the knowledge acquired by prior generations. By studying books, he does not have to start from rediscovering the wheel as the computer edge has placed in his hands the knowledge from all over the world on his finger tips. The value of acquiring a language for communication and for acquiring thoughts and facts should be duly recognized. It is this factor which enabled man to go from success to success.

Tender feelings have been the hallmark of humans. Poetry, scriptures, novels, articles and all such other literary collections have brought generation after generation face to face the expressions of earlier writers. Advancement of the civilization is to be judged by the prevalence of such emotional qualities in a society. The record of the previous century has been blemished by the occurrence of battles and wars. The 20th century has left the darkest record of cruel behaviour in human. The two world wars witnessed the worst that can happen to human beings.

There is a need to distinguish between compassion and pity. Pity is the feeling of sympathy aroused by a tragic circumstance. It comes and also this appears with the changes in the circumstances. Compassion, on the other hand, is a feeling of a permanent nature experienced towards other human beings and even all living beings of empathy. It is the capability of experiencing the pain and misery be underground which other people are undergone.

More advanced communities have greater compassion, great religions like Buddhism, Jainism, have compassion as their basic tenet. Their faith encompasses not only the human society but the entire living world. Jainism has in fact gone to the extent of caring for invisible, a normally ignored living species. The priests of Jainism wear a piece of cloth in front of their mouth for the fear that some ultra small form of animal life might enter into their mouth and get killed. Buddhism, on the other hand, does not show meticulousnes in avoiding oppression on animal life.

Religions have developed in different environments and conditions. Islam and Christianity took their roots in barren countries like the deserts of Middle East or in the extreme cold regions of Europe. The availability of food grain has been scarce in these parts of the world. Instead, animals thriving on the meager vegetation and limited supply of food grains have become the staple food of man in these regions. It is therefore noted that the religions like Judaism, Christianity and Islam support the idea of killing animals for sustaining human life. In India also some sects of Hinduism carried the tradition of sacrificing animals before the deity. Islam has gone a step further and has laid down that (Qurbani) or ritual slaughter of goats and lambs must be performed during bakra-eid by every devotee Muslim family. It is seen that many Muslims find it an honorous task to perform. In the barren desert regions of Middle East where Islam took its birth there was no way of surviving except by consuming meat of animals. The religions mentioned above do not lay emphasis on compassion to lower animals because of this factor.

✴ ✴ ✴

The Incidents Of The Killing Of A Dove & Reaction Of The Mother

Hunting has been accepted a way of sport and procuring for food. It is believed that man was a "hunter-gatherer" in the early stages of human evolution. The pre-historic rock-shelters in India and also elsewhere in the world depict scenes of hunting. Old scriptures of Hindu and other faiths contend description of hunting by rulers. This activity had full support of the society, perhaps because the dangerous carnivores were also taken care of by hunters there by protecting the cattle wealth and human lives. Since the beginning of the second half of 20th Century, hunting came to look down upon so many countries passed laws placing restriction on this sport. In fact, the protection of wild life has become a Hallmark of advanced societies making 'Shikaar' or hunting a matter of the past. This can be counted as a progressive step in the evolution of the human society.

During the period when hunting was in vogue the

pain and misery suffered by the wild animals was never taken into account. Tiger shooting was a creditable achievement for members of the higher society. Shooting wild bore and antelopes (like deer and stags etc.) were equally popular.

An elderly friend of my father, Mr. Naval Kishore, Dy. Collector describes to us a poignant experience of 'Shikaar'. When he shot down a dove, the young offspring of the dove (the fawn) remained standing staring at its dying mother instead of running away at the sound of the gun. The incident shook the hunter friend from the roots of his conscious. He gave up hunting thereafter. Though, it was a very prestigious and popular sport amongst senior civil servants. With the sound of the gun and falling of the mother dead, this fawn ('kkod) should have run away for his life after hearing sound of the gun but did not do so because of its affection for the mother. Mr. Naval Kishore was reminded of this tragic incident when his wife died and his children remained hovering around their dead mother. All in all the stoppage of

16

hunting as sport has certainly been a step forward in the compassionate development of human society.

His holiness, the Dalai Lama has been propagating that people should develop a compassionate outlook in their daily life. He has distinguished this from pity which is a temporary emotion generated by a tragic incident. Pity comes and goes away but the sentiments of compassion are to be nurtured as the hallmark of one's personality.

There is another side of this view the inveterate and cruel have gained upper hand over others by indulging in stark violence. The history of Muslim victories in India in historical times is an example of this one cannot easily forget. The bravery of Mata Gujari the wife of Gurunanak Dev and mother of Guru Govind Singh ji whose two adolescent sons were interred in a wall in her own presence by Aurangzeb. Due to lack of compassionate aliment in the religion, Islam, as it was practiced in those days, acts of brutality over nonbelievers of Islam population in general were quite frequent. By this way, they dominated the opponent Hindu community and established empires in this country.

The absence of compassion in Islam has, however, not helped in the evolution of Islamic world, which is strewn with internecine wars and battle, not to speak of minor incidents of scuffles. Recent historical events' illustrating this point is the down fall of Iraq. Saddam Hussain commanded power over tremendous oil-wealth. He had a strong army to support him with the help of which he could never annex Iraq's, Kuwait. He had been devoid of compassion. As a consequence he got a huge number of Shia Muslims massacred under his orders. The US forces ultimately occupied a rock and taught a lesson to Saddam Hussain by hunting him out of his hideout. He was tried for his cruel acts and ultimately hanged. The precious antique wealth of Iraq and its modern valuable possession, the oil-wealth, could not come to his rescue. The story of Saddam adds a

18

significant chapter to the progress of human civilization in the direction of compassionate humane behaviour.

✖ ✖ ✖

The World Of Literature – Record Of Tender Human Feelings

The birth of poetic sentiments:

Poetry enshrines within itself the tender sentiments of human beings. According to Sanskrit Scholars first poetic sentiment came into existence when Maharshi Valmiki saw a hunter shooting down a copulating loving couple. The first 'Shlok' of Sanskrit born out of intense feeling of pity which came out involuntarily out of the mouth of Maharshi Valmiki runs as follows:-

"मा निषाद् प्रतिष्ठान्तवम् अगमः शाश्वति समः,
यत्क्रौंच मिथुनादेकम् .... ।

The sensitivity required for a poetic creation is special to some rare individuals. It is not possible for an ordinary person to write poetry worth the name unless he gets inspired for such writing from within. Nature has gifted some human beings with the talent.

Epics like 'Ramayana' of Maharshi Valmiki and the Hindi "Ram Charit Manas" of Tulsidas are great examples of such creativity. These works of rare inspiration have guided the societies of their belonging to great heights in humane attitude.

✖ ✖ ✖

The Evolutionary Value Of Faith

It is a matter of curiosity to find out whether faith has helped masses in achieving peace and progress. Men achieved results by their concrete efforts in worldly matters. It remains to be seen whether the inspiration given by faith makes them better achievers.

On the micro level we find that those who stick to their faith and draw support and solace from their faith have gone into to become more successful then others. On the macro level this test yields some valuable results.

There have been two major powers, Soviet Union and the USA. One of them, the Soviet Union had the policy of totally eliminating religion as a faith amongst its citizens. This nation drew inspiration from the book "Das Capital" in which Karl Marx wrote that religion is the opiate of man. He decried religious faith and as a result of which Christianity or Islam was banished from that country. It is noteworthy that this nation made rapid progress in the field of science and economic affairs under the Communist regime. It surpassed USA in matters of space exploration and defense preparedness. Its aggressive postures frightened America and the West European countries so much so that they started adopting majors to count rate to growing Soviet influence a cold war ensued. Schemes like Marshal Plan were brought in Western European countries by US to check the Russian threat.

Over the years, however, Soviet Union started lagging behind. The United States of America on the other hand made stendy progress and successfully countered threat from communism. Two nations owing elisions to two different faiths were a competition with each other. The motto recorded in the US constitution declares **"In god, we trust"**. USA is thus a country which believes in god as an article of national faith. No none-believer or atheist can hold any national level office. It may be mentioned that in India, such people have the option

23

of taking oath in the name of god or making a solemn affirmation. In the latter case belief in god or any such super natural power is not a necessary condition.

United India was divided between Pakistan and India on 15th August 1947 on the basis of religion. In fairness the rest of India should have been named as Hindustan instead, this country was declared as a "Secular State". This meant that there was no official religion of this country. The concept of secularism was borrowed from Machiavelli of Italy. Italy and the rest of Europe has been suffering at the hands of religious leaders, like the Pope of Vatican City. The interference of Pope in the national affairs of European countries was resented by many countries. England got away from the yoke of the Pope instead, England declared the British Monarch as the head of their Church. Amongst many titles adorning the King of England is the titled "Defender of Faith". No wonder England prospered and attained the top position in the world affairs when they had the secular powers and the ecclesiastic functions combined in their Queen and King. Allegiance to the monarch also carried with itself the faith in the divinity of their King.

In India also Kings were looked upon as incarnates of God. "The divine right of Kingship was the ruling sentiments before the advent of democracy in modern form". In many States like Rewa the head of the State was the 'Rajadhiraj', Bhagwan Ramchandra the ruling king was his Sarbarakaar or Agent to perform the duties of kingship on behalf of the presiding deity. During the Dussera festival the royal procession use to be headed by the chariot (or car) of the Rajadhiraj, while that of the Maharaja followed behind. All the treaties agreement etc. were signed by the ruler on behalf of the Rajadhiraj. This brought in the factor of faith amongst the subject of the ruler towards the State.

The 'Darshan' (or a glimpse) of the Ruler was an important routine in the lives of the devout subject of the Ruler. An extreme case of this blind faith in the divine powers of the ruler was in the daily routine of devout Hindu subjects. These people would not take food or even water before they had a glimpse of Aurangzeb. Many such people living in the Chandni-Chowk area of Delhi used to wait for the appearance of Aurangzeb at his Zarokha (window) before beginning their day. Thus, even a heartless cruel emperor like Aurangzeb received obedience from his subjects.

Divinity bestowed upon the Rulers made the task of administration easy. As a person feared not only the right of the King to control and punish his erring subjects but the subjects bowed down to his command due to religious faith in his divinity. This factor brought discipline in the society even when the Rulers were not fit people to rule over the kingdom.

The orderliness and discipline instilled in the society by the faith in the divine powers of the kings brought about development in the society. This led the foundation of peaceful coexistent amidst citizens who could then engage themselves in constructive activities. This let to improvement in the economic conditions of the society and also encouraged progress in the field of art, literature and scientific research. The evolutionary value of such a benevolent influence should not be underestimated. While societies torn by lawlessness made no progress. Countries like England, on the other hand, took giant steps towards world domination during the peaceful era of queen Elizabeth-I. A strong handed ruler who was also the head of the Church of England guided the fate of the country to unparallel heights. Institutions like a trading Corporation, East India Company came into existence during this period This Company established an Emperor in India which lasted for about a century and half.

Not only does Faith inspire countries but great man like Mahatma Gandhi produced miraculous results by their devoted allegiance to their faith. The Mahatma had staunch faith in truth and non-violence alongside faith in Geeta and Ramayan. Saint Narsi Mehta's verses had

27

sustained him through the struggle against the mighty British rule. The Bhajan, "वैष्णव जन तो तेणे कहिये जे पीड़ पराई जाणै रे" and "रघुपति राघव राजाराम, पतित पावन सीताराम" were his source of strength. It was difficult to imagine that a Bar-at-law educated in England and settled for several years in South Africa could take the leadership in India to uproot the British rule so firmly establish in India.

Twenty years ago, on December 25, 1991, Mikhail Gorbachev resigned as president of the Soviet Union, declaring the office extinct and dissolving the Union of Soviet Socialist Republics (USSR), a massive communist empire that had existed since 1922. The USSR had been in a long economic stagnation when Gorbachev came to power in 1985. In order to bring about change, he introduced several reforms, including perestroika (economic restructuring) and glasnost (openness).

Glasnost opened the floodgates of protest and many republics made moves toward independence, threatening the continued existence of the USSR. In August of 1991, a group of Communist Party hardliners frustrated by the separatist movement attempted to stage a coup. They quickly failed due to a massive show of civil resistance -- but the already-faltering government was destabilized even further by the attempt. By December of 1991, 16 Soviet republics had declared their independence, and Gorbachev handed over power to Russian president Boris Yeltsin, ending the USSR.

Judging a human being by his ability to bring about revolutionary changes we can trace the evolutionary process which endowed the evolved individuals with extraordinary powers.

The rational human being proceeds on the coolly calculated steps of the results of his efforts. Those, however, who are driven by the force of their faith achieve more than what a rationalist expects to achieve. For instance the Battle-Cry of the fighting forces induces extraordinary bravery in the soldiers. They achieve wonderful results when they are driven by their respective faiths.

The extreme and rather it-advised case is of Islamic faith held by the extremists of the organization called Al-Qaeda. The members of this sinister organization hold out promises of extraordinary reward in paradise to those who lay down their lives in pursuance of the terrorist's objectives of the Al-Qaeda. A news item appearing in the Internet is enclosed herewith Appendix- to illustrate to how nebulous dreams are woven to capture the young "Faithful" followers of Islam. The youngsters who are so motivated believe that there is the existence of a heavenly word in which all the lustful luxuries of the world are made available to them on performing foolhardy acts of terrorism. Such misplace trust in faith has brought down the value of this faith as an activator of benevolent. Faith is thus, capable of being used as a tool for good or for bad.

When put to a taste for its evolutionary value. The course of faith is evenly balanced between its good and bad consequences. Ultimately a rational approach garnered with a touch of reasonably rational faith is the best course of action to be followed by individual societies or nations. The Nazi Government under the leadership of Hitler perpetrated unbelievable acts of cruelty on the Jews living in Germany. This had disastrous result.

Such acts of madeness, driven by a detestable

Appendix

Three day strike Al Qaeda to go on strike, Muslim suicide bombers in Britain are set to begin a three-day strike next Monday in a dispute over the number of virgins they are entitled to in the afterlife. Emergency talks with Al Qaeda have so far failed to produce an agreement

The unrest began last Tuesday when Al Qaeda announced that the number of virgins a suicide bomber would receive after this death will be cut by 25% this April from 72 to only 60.

The rationale for the cut was the increase in recent years of the number of suicide bombings and a subsequent shortage of virgins in the afterlife.

The suicide bombers' union, the British Organization of Occupational Martyrs responded with a statement that this was unacceptable to its members and immediately balloted for strike action. General Secretary Abdullah Amir told the press, "Our members are literally working themselves to death in the cause of Jihad. We don't ask for much in return but to be treated like this is like a kick in the teeth".

Speaking from his shed in Tipton in the West Midlands in which he currently resides, an Al Qaeda chief executive explained, "We sympathize with our workers' concerns but Al Qaeda is simply not in a position to meet their demands. They are simply not accepting the realities of modern-day Jihad in a competitive marketplace. Thanks to Western depravity, there is now a chronic shortage of virgins in the afterlife. It's a straight choice between reducing expenditure and laying people off. I don't like cutting wages but I'd hate to have to tell 3000 of my staff that they won't be able to blow themselves up."

Representatives for the union in, Essex, Glasgow and also in Australia stated that they would be unaffected as there are no virgins in these areas anyway.

Apparently the drop in the number of suicide bombings has largely been put down to the emergence of the Scottish singing star, Susan Boyle. Now that Muslims know what a virgin looks like, they are not so keen on going to paradise.

(British Organization of Occupational Martyrs (or BOOM)

adherent to faith should be opposed by the whole world.

The United States of America has taken steps to prevent the propagation of such religious faiths which are considered unhealthy for their society in the long run. A glaring example of such action is the deportation of Osho from America. The mystic tenets of Bhagwan Rajneesh also called Osho have many such elements which may not for the good of the society is long run. His preaching of "Sambhog Se Samadhi Tak" (i.e. from voluptuous practices to eternal bliss) is always likely to create licentious tendencies in the society. The entire social fabrics based on the principle of having families bonded together by a solemn vow of sacred marriage are the hallmark of a normal society. The children born of such relationship have a secure and stable life. Letting loose the social and moral bindings can result in chaotic social conditions. The USA authorities lost no time in realizing this fact. They took the extreme steps of extermination Bhagwan Rajneesh from the USA. All nation's of the do world the preserved religious and social structure of their countries against such faiths.

The 'Faith' In Action

There is no proof to show how actions supported by belief in the right type of faiths lead to better results in a human being. It is possible that some hormones are secreted in the human body when the motivation due to faith takes place. Studies have shown that the Adrenal gland and the Thyroid glands do affect the activity of men. The co-relation between adherence to a faith and activation of these two endow-crime glands has been a matter of conjecture. Some experimental evidence needs to be brought into light on the subject. In the absence of such clear evidence we may take recourse to empirical studies of certain population to see if faith has brought about a strong motivation for better achievements. These studies are to be based on the whole populations living in a particular region.

Basing our observations on the success of different nations one can conclude that the United States of America has achieved high, nearly the highest, level of

progress. This is a nation which functions on faith. Its
motivation is derived from worlds of it Governmental
emblem **"In God, we trust"**. The nation which was
trying to compete with America was the Soviet Union
which disintegrated into several small republics. In
recent years its remnant portion, Russia has lagged
far behind the United States. Religion was banished
from Soviet Union for more than half century. The
comparison between these two countries, which are the
most prominent powers of the world leads to the belief
that faith in a religion has given better motivation to
the people of the US. Devoid of any religious fervor,
the people of Soviet Union fail to achieve better results
than those of US. The absence of profit motive in the
communist society is also one of the factors responsible
will for low rate of success.

Coming nearer home, one can identify certain
communities of our country as being more enterprising
an economically successful as compared to others.
In an empirical way it may be safely stated that the

people of Gujarat and Punjab have done better than people of other States. The population of the Gujarat is predominantly Hindu and has a strong faith in the Krishna cult. There usual greeting each other is "Jai Shrikrishna". The community has come in for adverse social activities during the course of the notorious riots of the year 2002. However, condemnable this may be, the fact of the devoted activity of the people of Gujarat is well established. Not only in India, but the people of Gujarat have been exceedingly successful abroad. In east Africa, as also in the US, the Gujarati's have entrenched themselves as leaders in business. Their way of life is as much business like as it is attach to devotion. The Islamic cult of Daudi Bohara's hailing from the Kutch region of Gujarat is one of the advanced entrepreneurs in local business in urban areas. These people adhere strictly to the commandments of the leaders of the community. Theirs is a well neat closed-circuit religious sect presided over by a leader whose word is law for them. The community pools together its financial resources and comes to the rescue of their weaker members as and when necessary. They maintain a very decent living. The social interaction is mostly confined to their own community. The Kutchee-Bohara community is one of the most trusted commercial communities of India. Besides these people, the Gujarati traders of all other communities have a record of achieving grand success in their business ventures.

The other economically successful business community is of the people of Punjab. The most successful part of this community consists of Sikh entrepreneurs. The adherent to the religious cult of 'Khalsa' found amongst the Sikhs is exemplary. They continue to maintain the command of their Guru, Guru Gobind Singh, at the cost of associated discomfort. The observance of keeping *Kesh* (long hair), Kutchcha (under wear), Kripan (dagger), Kangha (comb) and Kada (a steal bracelet to be worn in the right hand) strictly followed by the devout Sikhs. Maintaining long hair with 'Pugri' on the head must be a matter of serious discomfort in hot and humid climates like that of Mumbai or Assam.

They still continue to maintain the ordained way of life.

The community, Parsees living in Gujarat and Mumbai has a total strength of just 1,10,000 in the world. Their contribution in the independence struggle and the industrialization of country has been unique and far beyond the contribution normally expected from such as small numbers.Dada Bhai Nourojee became a member of the British Parliament during the British rule. Sir Jamshedjee Nisarwanjee Tata setup the 'Tata Steel' plant in Jamsedpur. He also harnessed the waters of the Western Ghat for power generation to be supplied to Bombay. The house of Tata's has been the most trusted and successful name of industry not only in India but around the whole world. Tata's have acquired car making plants of Jaguar Land rover and of England. Due to continuous in-breeding and abstention from marriages, this most advanced community is dwindling in numbers. The succession in the magnificent house of Tata's has been going on through adoptions. This demographic disaster should be matter of great concern to our nation.

Another highly successful community is of Iyers residing near Pallickal (Palghat). People like Seshan former Election Commissioner of India have proved their work in public life. Shivait's by faith they are devoted workers and hard task masters. Menon's of Kerala are well known for their successful enterprise.

Coming to the North again the Kashmiri Pandits have contributed a lot to the national effort during and after independence struggle. Leaders like Motilal Nehru, Pt. Jawaharlal Nehru and Indira Gandhi have made historical contributions to the progress of the country. Pandit Jawaharlal was, of course, a great rationalist with scientific temper and, so far as a known, did not attach himself to any religious faith. Indira Gandhi had visited a few Hindu shrines and was reportedly attached to Hinduism. Her greatest historical contribution is decimation of East Pakistan and creation of Bangladesh in its place.

◼ ◼ ◼

The Psychic Factors Affecting Human Nature

From times immemorial, the human kind has sought refuge in the benevolence of a supernatural power. It is doubtful if god created man but it is more appropriate to say that man created god. Besides his own-power and strength the humans beings have always invoked the powers and blessing of a superpower. This led to the creation of releases faiths. These reasons have supported the idea that there is a supernatural power which regulates the affairs of the universe. Discoveries made by scientist have gone on solving the mysteries of the physical world beginning from the creation of universe, the stars and planets up to the evolution of life and ultimately of the human society. Even when a rational explanation is available for various activities of the nature human being have reposed faith in a power which is beyond these explanations. In most of the religious faiths of the world it is postulated that the super power associated with each religion can be invoked for seeking mental peace and added vigour for one's efforts.

There are hardly die-hard nationalist in the world. There was a whole land mass, the Soviet Union, where religious faith had been banned and rational society was sought to be created. It was perhaps because of the natural inclination of humans towards a divine force that this experiment did not succeed over a long period. The Soviet Union got disintegrated into Russia and a number of Islamic Republics of Central Asia. The Church which had been banished from the Soviet Union staged a gradual comeback. Freedom of religion was slowly granted to the people.

There is a story illustrating the way in which human nature works in the matter of rational thinking. The story goes that 4 men were travelling in a boat when a dangerous storm came over the sky. When the boat became shaky and appeared to the sinking, the believers in their religions starting praying to their God. The Hindu invoked the blessings of the Hindu deities, the

Muslim those of Allah and the Christian Lord Jesus.
The forth man was an atheist. At long last he also rose
in hand and cried "Oh God, if there is any God, save
my soul if there is any soul. The atheist do not believed
in the existence of God or soul, but when faced with
a drastic situation they also yield to the view which
recognized the presence of both these entities.

The Good And The Bad Of It
Good:
- People have drowned strength from their faiths
  and performed almost impossible tasks.
- They have followed a moral path dictated by
  their religion.
- It has united the followers of the same faith into
  a coherent group.

The Bad Points:
The religious faith has been mutually exclusive.
They have been intolerant of other faiths. Lot of blood-

shed has taken place due to clash of religions.

In Hindu faith there is belief in the theory of rebirth of soul. The poverty and the backwardness of the depress classes of Hindu society has been often justified by saying that these people had done evil deeds in their past life due to which they are suffering now. Having undergone the ordeal of present days the deprivation they would be entitled to a happy and prosperous life in their next berth. Such a pretext to keep the poor and down trodden section of the Hindu society is a condemnable use of the theory of the transmigration of the soul. Fortunately, such beliefs are being gradually discarded.

Human society has always depended on its faith in powers beyond the material world. It is a part of man's nature to draw solace and strength from an entity which is supposed to come to his rescue in a period of distress and add vigor to his efforts when he is exerting. The physical tangible existence of such entity is not the issue with most people. They repose their trust in such heavenly powers. As this yields rich dividends, faith rules the human mind in a compulsive way.

A vast majority of humanity is attached to one or the other religions. Children's are conditioned to belief in their chosen faith. They gradually develop dependence on their religion for their upright moral behavior and also seek solace and mental strength.

It is said that man does not live by bread alone. Besides his physical existence, man has a strong mental existence. Supported by his physical conditions, the factor of humanity, the essence of being a man is derived from his mental makeup and emotional reactions. In advanced societies the creature comforts and the essentials of living are so readily available that the mental activity of man has become the prime factor in deciding the quality of life.

As man evolved from humanoids several anatomical and physiological developments have taken place to make man the most successful product of nature. Some of these are listed below:

1.   The Erect Posture
The ancestors of a man descended from the trees and started living on the ground. Here man developed the capacity to use only two-Legs out of his four extremities for locomotion. This releases the other two upper extremities-the hands for various activities.

2.   The Opposable Thumb
Unlike the animals, man is able to use his thumb with other four fingers for the purpose of holding things. This factor called the "opposable thumb" made the way for art and culture. All future developments of the human race were made possible by this hither to less recognized fact.

3.   The Binocular Vision.
Most of the animals are able to see on one side only with their eye. In the case of human beings the eyes

shifted from the sides of the head to the forehead with the results that man could see up to a long distance with both the eyes. This enabled him to judge the distances and have a proper perspective of the surroundings.

4. Increase Cranial Capacity.

Unlike the early humanoids whose brain capacity was around 700 to 800cc developed his cranial capacity to 1100cc to 1200cc. Further, this increase capacity came in the forehead of man. Instead of having a sloping forehead as is the case with apes, man has a protruding forehead. The newly developed part of the brain located in the frontal part of the brain case contains the thinking part of humans. While the biological functions of the body are regulated by the back portion of the brain and spinal cord, the memory, thinking process, emotions and such others high level mental activity take place because of the activity of the front lobe of the brain.

5. Evolution Of Language.

A very vital step in human evolution has been

the advent of Language. Once man started using communication with each other, a giant step in human affairs was achieved. The language enabled not only the communication between contemporary associates but also brought forth the knowledge accumulated over several generations to the descendants, thus nobody was required to rediscover the wheel or burning of fire. Each generation built upon the knowledge gained by the previous generation and thus brought the human society to its present hi-tech level.

Language thus serves the purpose of a channel of communication and also of the storage of accumulated wisdom and knowledge.

In this respect human differs from the members of the other animal world. Each generation of other animals learns how to live and survive in its own life time. They do not have the benefit of learning from accumulated experiences nor can they pass on the benefit of their knowledge to their progeny.

49

Language has thus assumed place of great importance in human affairs. The teaching of languages takes a prime place in education. Linguistic minorities clamor for their recognition. People speaking the same language aggregate together, eg. we in India have formed States on linguistic bases.

In due course of time language has become the repository of works of science, arts and literature.

The course of evolution in the animal kingdom has been through a process comprising a struggle for existence and the survival of the fittest. On the other hand, in human beings competition has been replaced by cooperation. It is the cooperative effort of generations after generations that have made the scientific and social progress of man possible. Further, there is a social evolution instead of individual evolution. The society makes progress and the individuals comprising the society stand to benefit by it. Not only the fit and successful individuals are the beneficiaries of this evolutionary process but also the unfit members of the society are helped in the struggle for existence, the society ensures the survival of its weaker sections. Communities suffering neglect and deprivation for centuries have been brought at par with the advanced part of the society by a process of granting reservation for their members so that they can come at par with the members of advanced society. The modern society does not ruthlessly eliminate its weaker (unfit) members but takes upon itself the task of their happy survival.

Societies differ in the content of compassion in their tenets. Buddhism and Jainism excel in their devotion to the sentiment of compassion. While Buddhism has been quite practical in its prescribed code of treating animals allowing the killing of animals for food in hospitable areas like Tibet, Jainism has gone onto lay down that all forms of life including microscopic creatures ought to be given protection. The saints belonging to Jain religion wear a piece of cloth in front of their mouth so that minute creature do not inter the mouth and die. There is no denying that followers of this rigid faith have been, by and large financially well off. Their regimented lives have instilled austerity and self discipline in their lives they have been so successful in establishing their faith that a new category of food is now known by the name of this religion. In the international flights touching India especially those touching India serve "Jain Food" besides veg and non-veg menu. The follower of this religion has turned the Jain community into very successful traders. In practice, it is observed that Jain's have remained vegetarian and teetotalers, a factor making for their success. It is however worthy of note that Jainism is a "Unishwarwadi" (Not believing in God) religion. Their own beliefs and practices do keep them very strictly attached to their faith.

Islam is characterized by its emphasis on equality amongst followers of this religion. According to some historians large scale conversions from Hinduism to Islam took place due to the prevalent sentiment of equality in that religion. The following couplet conveys the sense of equality prevailing in Islam "**Ekhi saf me Khade ho gaye mehmood or Aayaz, na koi banda raha na koi bandanawaz**". During namaz both Mehmood the master and Aayaz, the slave stood in the same line then there was no one as the master or slave.

It is, on the other hand, a faith which is highly intolerant of the existence of other religions; so much so that, the nonbelievers in Islam called by a generic name *Kafirs* deserve death penalty at the hands of devout Muslim. Further, those who perform the act of putting kafirs to death earn the title of Ghazi. With its ruthless ways Islam succeeded in spreading its wings from Mecca in Saudi Arab up to Indonesia. One of the compulsory duties of a firm believer in Islam is to perform the act of sacrifice during Bakrid. Slaughtering a goat or lamb on this occasion is a compulsory duty imposed on Muslims. Due to this practice Muslims are attuned to killing there adversaries ruthlessly. Not only this, the propensity to cause deaths on a large scale has been found to be a factor in their nature. There is a historical event of the wholesale massacre of the Hindu population of Delhi city by a Muslim invader, Nadir Shah. This incident took place just because a few soldiers of Nadir Shah's army had been reportedly harassed by some citizens of Delhi. In recent times mass scale killing of innocent people has taken place as in the case of 9/11 carnage on the Twin Towers of New York. The man responsible for this was Osama-Bin Laden who has since been shot dead by the helicopter-board secret service agents of the U.S. A few thousand innocent citizens of the New York City were killed by the attack of two passenger Aircrafts on these towers. In fact, besides these two planes there were other two passenger Aircrafts, which were used by Osama on this occasion. One of them hit the military headquarters of U.S. The Pentagon Campus. The other Aircraft was to hit the White House but this did not happen as the pilots of this plane announced to the innocent passengers that they were all about to die when the plane would crash on its target. The brave passengers of this aircraft then rose to fight with the pilots and averted the falling of the plane on the white house. They however, bravely laid down their lives to save the presidential abode because the plane crashed due to the scuffle with the pilots.

The unprovoked attack on innocent people in India by the use of explosive devices has taken a heavy toll of life. The worst incident has been attack on 26th Sept 2008 at the famous Taj Mahal hotel and two other similarly famous spots of Mumbai. Those who came to cause this traveled by boat from Pakistan with the aid of Islamic terrorist organization set up by the Pak Govt. There have been frequent incidents in the Middle East in which Muslims themselves have been made victims due to sectarian enmity. Thus Islamic faith has turned out to be violence-prone. There is of-course, a branch known as Sufi sect which, believes in peaceful observance of religion.

✖ ✖ ✖

Mahatma Gandhi And His Faith

Mahatma Gandhi was born as Mohan Das Karam Chand Gandhi in Gujrat where Jainism had a great influence. Though not a Jain himself, he adopted the principals of Ahimsa and Satya (Non-violence and Truth) as tenets of his Hindu belief. He spent four years of his early life from the age of 17 up to his passing the Bar-at-law examination. He continued to follow his pursuit of spirituality. Having given a word to his mother of abstaining from wine, women, and non-vegetarian food he was encouraged to delve deep into spiritual thoughts and practices. This struggle continued when he moved out as a practicing lawyer to South Africa. The title of his autobiography, "My Experiments with Truth" contains a vivid account of struggle that had been going on in his mind all these years. He became a firm believer that ends do not justify the means. In other words, he came to the conclusion that good results can be achieved only by implying proper and sacrosanct means. He therefore ruled out violence as a way of achieving India's freedom.

It was another belief of the Mahatma that there is an inherent strength in Truth and Non-violence to bend down the opponents. For this purpose his methodology came to be known as 'Satyagraha'. This was in short a method of bringing the wrong doers to the right path by sticking to the path of Truth and Non-violence. His autobiography, "My Experiments with truth" is in fact a record of his experiences of persisting in the strength of his standing by what he believed to be the Truth. His ultimate success came when he was able to approve the deeply entrenched British rule in India. He used his long spells of fasting (Upvas) to achieve his goals which were supported by his faith in truth.

It is a matter of conjecture whether there is really a mechanism by which truth can prevail over non-truth. Our nation has adopted the motto "Satya Mev Jayate" which means Truth alone triumphs. On taking a very broad view about the inherent power behind Truth one may say that normally things which are beneficial to the society and which enjoy the approval and support of the masses go on to be implemented by the force of journal approval behind them.

It is difficult to arrive at the absolute Truth. What is truth (i.e. fair and right) for one may not be so for some others. Sacrificing a goat on the occasion of Bakrid may be the truth for the followers of Islam but may be a sacrilege for the follower of Jainism. Instead of getting involved into such intricacy of philosophy, Mahatma Gandhi chose his path by a common sense decision on the subject. He postulated that truth is god. How firm and deep seated was his faith in this believe that he was prepare to stake his life for what he believe to be the truth. The power and strength that he drew from such ardent faith gave him the energy to fight against the British Rule. This was a unique example in the history of the world that a mighty empire has disappeared from a Country by the non-violent insistence on Truth.

Strangely enough Mahatma failed to exercise the same Moral Power when the question of the partition of the country arose. He, who had undertaken fast unto death or for a long period of 21 days in the past turned away from the truth that partitioning an ancient great country like India on religious bases was against all the norms of truth. Instead of preventing this catastrophe with his moral force, he chose to withdraw to Bengal, engaging in matters of lesser consequence. The achievement of the freedom of the country for which credit must go in a major part to him has been overshadowed by the woes and wails of partition. The bases of dividing the country were whether in any province the majority of population was of Hindu's or of Muslim's. It was never taken into account as to what would be the fate of the minorities left in these provinces. No mechanism of preventing atrocities by the majority over the minority had been laid out. In retrospect, it is indeed shocking to realize that the best brains of the country, viz. leaders like Mahatma Gandhi, Jawaharlal Nehru, Maulana Azad to name only few did not realize the calamities that the

59

partition of the country would bring about. Firstly, there was immediate disaster in the shape of communist strife accompanying the division of the provinces on religious bases. Then there was unplanned and haphazard transfer of population with lakhs of people being uprooted from their ancient homes and hearths. In the case of north-eastern India none of these leader cast a glance on how communications will be maintained between the states of Assam and neighborhood and the rest of India. Arrangements for rail and road communication from these states via East Pakistan to the rest of India were never given any consideration resulting in the near total isolation of these areas. The new route to North-East via Naxalbari and Siligudi was hurriedly built to keep the contact alive if the faith of the people, Hinduism or Islam, has caused atrocious consequences; the example is in the heartless partition of the country.

The bottom line is that the Mahatma shut his eyes from such stark realities and allowed them to happen.

◗ ◗ ◗

Focused And Unfocused Faiths

Religions like Islam which are based on the revelations and preaching of one individual, hold the faith of the followers in a focused manner. In the following two lines the sense of Islam has been condensed La ilahi Illilaha Mohammed Rasulilaha (there is only one God and Hazrat Mohammed is his only representative). Similarly, Christianity derives it teachings from what Jesus Christ preached. These sermons have been recorded in the Holy Bible.

In the case of Islam there was a division of a Religion in two main branches, Sunnies and Shias. In Christianity similar division took place by the introduction of the reformist religion Protestantism. Now there are two branches of Christianity, the Catholics who believed in the word of Pop of Rome and the other branch, the Protestants who are divided in several smaller denominations like the Church of England with British monarch as its head. The church of north and south India, the seventh day Adventists mission and so on. While the Catholics believe in a small measure in idol worship of Mother Mary, the Protestants keep no such faith in any idol. From the practical and utilitarian point of view, Christianity has been the most successful faith so far. Compassion towards humanity forms the hardcore of this religion which has the largest numbers of followers in the world.

The ancient Hinduism called the Sanatan Dharma has a Pantheon of a large number of Deities, the principal once being Brahma, Vishnu and Mahesh of these only Vishnu and Mahesh are actively worshiped. Besides these three chief centers of faith there is a large no of Deities who are the object of devotion and worship for Hindus. The incarnations of God prominently, Ram and Krishna have enjoyed the highest devotional fervor. In the end four lines of the Hindu faith have come to stay, the Vaishnavas (covering Ram and Krishna) Shivoits with lord Shiva at the center and the shakt with powerful female deities, Durga, Kali, Chamunda and others.

Islam and Christianity have congregational worship where as Hinduism is by enlarge believer in isolated individual prayers. Sikhism is a branch of Hindu faith and several other similar religious denominations have taken to Group prayers. This system of worship keep the community well knit and well protected against the onslaught of other communities. It must be remembered that religions thrive on their being separate in beliefs and methods of worship from each other. The multiplicity of Deities has blurred vision of the Hindus. Their beliefs are divided due to lack of congregational worship, the unity found amongst Muslim, Christian and Sikhs are not noticeable amongst Hindus in short they are an amorphous lot. The Hindu psyche is therefore highly individualistic. There are occasions when they act in unison but, by enlarge their thinking is individualistic. This was a cause of weakness when Hinduism was pitched against other more aggressive religions like the

Islam.

The faith of individuals, however, was staunch and unshaken during these times of crisis. There was a deep seated faith in the powers of righteousness. They believed in conforming to the classical rules of battles. They would rather die facing the enemy than retreat from the battle field. Thus they always fought dharma-yudh giving a fair chance to their opponents. This system of fighting was good enough when both the warring groups observed the same rules of conducting a battle. The raiders coming from the north-western Islamic countries however observed none-of- these classic rules of battle.

When Shivaji came on the scene, he realized that there was no point in fighting a Dharma-yudh (or war according to the religiously laid down war rules) with those people, (vidharmis) who did not follow the rules of a Dharma-Yudhh. He then handled the enemies in the way they deserved to be dealt with. Shivaji resorted to Guerilla warfare, attacking the enemy when the enemy was weak and withdrew to safety when the enemy was strong. He had no compunction in attacking the enemy from behind or at night. He believed that invaders had no business of fighting on our soil and that they deserved no protection of the Dharma-yudh, war conducted according to the religious scriptures. In this way he overcame a great handicap of the Hindu faith. The foreign invaders used to be inveterate fighters, the Indian defenders on the other hand had bound themselves by the enceintes traditional rules of fighting. Had the European powers the Dutch, the Portuguese, the French and ultimately the British had not entered in the fray, Shivaji would have won the independence for the country from foreign invaders in his own times.

✘ ✘ ✘

Different Objects of Faith

Apart from faith in religious tenets their have been other articles of faith. The most prominent amongst these is the trust palace by Mahatma Gandhi on Truth and Non-violence. He had implicit faith in the efficacy of these principles. Also related to these faiths was the idea that the means employed to achieve an object should be fair and even pious. He believed that ends do not justify the means. How so ever grand the objective may be to be achieved, it was necessary according to him to employ only just and fair means to achieve those goals. The withdrawal of agitation against the British Government when it was at its zenith because of the Chouri-Choura incident is a great historical example of his firm faith in non-violence. The event of an attack by freedom fighter on the police personnel at village Chouri-Choura in U.P. deeply hurt him. He declared the suspension of the entire National mobilization against the British Government. It is recorded by many contemporary historians that this act did not go well with the highly motivated public of India. The Muslim League, in particular, could not countenance this action of the Mahatma and gradually withdrew itself from the independence movement launched by Mahatma Gandhi. The Independence of the country could, perhaps, been listen by a decades. Agitation was not brought to a jolting heart due to the conscientious objection of Mahatma.

Mahatma Gandhi's faith is the efficacy of truth and non-violence was very deep sited. His device of Satyagrah was founded on this faith. He had a fun faith that by employing the moral pressure of fair and chaste issues, the opposite party could be forced to agree to the demands. He had successfully tried this device during his agitation in South Africa. Rejecting the mixture of violent and non-violent beings propagated by his predecessors like Lokmanya Tilak. He placed implicit faith in non-violent ways of agitating against the British rule.

It is not worthy to his principles and methodology succeeded against the British because of the sensitivity of the British Government towards his non-violent agitation. In fact, both were equally matched. T he Mahatma could not have achieved the goals by these principles against a totalitarian regime. The Nazis of Germany would not have accepted any of his demands put force by in non-violence agitation. The achievement of India's independence against mighty power like the British has a great historical achievement of faith. More than any religious belief, Gandhiji's adherence to his faith in Satya (truth) and Ahimsa (Non-violence) achieved a success of faith of the highest historical magnitude.

◼ ◼ ◼

Hitler's Misplaced Faith In Aryan Superiority

The name of the German dictator, Adolph Hitler will go down in history as one who was the greatest enemy of human kind. When he came to power in Germany in the late nineteen thirties, he cynically indulged in putting into practice his theory of the superiority of Aryan race. The Germans belonged according to him to a superior Aryan race. The people of the Anglo-Saxon and the Nordic races of England and other western European countries were considered by him to be much inferior and deserving of being ruled by the Aryans. Misguided by his obsession he mobilized the might of Germany to throw the world into the flames of a cruel war lasting for six years, nineteen thirty nine to nineteen forty five. Such ardent faith in a wrong notion created untold misery in the world.

Hitler's wrath was particularly directed towards the Jews living in Austria and Germany. Driven by a frenzied faith in a belief he resorted to utterly inhuman ways of eliminating the Jews population of these countries. This is an instance of mass scale fanaticism based on improper and inhuman tenets of faith.

The machinery of the State was put to use perpetrating unbelievable acts of cruelty on a mass scale. Nearer home, The Direct Action Day Programme of the Muslim League Govt. of Bengal committed similar carnage at Calcutta under the guidance of the then Chief Minister Suhara Warthi in the year just preceding. Trust in the Islamic faith is the root of this colossal human tragedy.

There are often reports of acts of utter inhumanness driven by faith. Several young and tender children have been sacrificed before the deities due to such misguided trust in pseudo-religious faiths. Similarly old helpless women have been put to death in the mistaken belief that such women were witches. They were held responsible for the miseries suffered by some people of village due to lack of education and rational thinking in the villagers. Reasons like lack of education and rational thinking are behind such acts of cruelty. All this leads to the confusion that "Faith" is not an unmixed evil. If it vitiates the faculty of balanced rational thinking, it can lead to totally condemnable results. The history of the world is replete with events in which humanity have been sacrificed at the alter of a fanatic belief women have been Burt elite. Galileo had been put to death for putting forth the idea that the earth revolves around the sun and not that the sun revolves around the earth which was the belief of his contemporary religious leaders.

Thus, faith has its value in human affairs provided the object of faith is rational and humane; otherwise, it can lead to disastrous results.

■ ■ ■

Faith In 'God-Men'

Besides faith in structured religions, some individual have commanded the faith of a large section of community. In recent years, there has been a proliferation of such persons who are loosely referred as 'God-Men'. Among them one can count saint like Shridi-Saibaba. Shri Satya Saibaba of Puttapati, etc. The physical presence of such saints or the shrines commemorating their memory have drawn a great devotion from their follows. They command better obeisance from their devotees. Within the framework of a larger religious faith, such individuals grip the attention of their followers, because of the existence of local devotional groups. The devotees claim miraculous powers of such 'God-Men' and repose. Such devotees have a deep-seated ardent faith in them which is rare to find amongst the followers of the wider generic religion. There are numerous sentences of various places where their devotees congregate regularly. A great quality of Christianity and the Islam is their system of group worship in Churches and Mosques. The prayer-centres of these God-men fulfill the need of group worship.

Some exceptions have also come to notice where the devotees have been misled towards blind faith. (The case of Shri Nirmaljit Singh Narula who later converted himself "Nirmal Baba" is, perhaps, an example of such misplaced faith.) Several religions do-owe their origin to individual saints. Buddhism came into being on the basis of the preaching of Gautam, the Buddha. Christianity began with Jesus Christ and Islam began with Hazarat Mohammad Paigamber.

The world of faiths is always a matter of conjecture. The need felt by human beings for a source of strength and solace beyond the physical world drove humanity into searching for objects of faith. According to some thinkers, the concept of God originated from the psychology of man. Human beings looked upon their father to be the source of their protection and well being. This childhood image of father did not stand the test of truth as the children grieve into adulthood. They, therefore, invented in imaginary personality as their father in heaven. This imaginary personality was presumed to be endowed with powers far beyond the capability of a human father. The concept of an almighty deity to whom individuals could approach for meeting their needs of protection and one who could grant them their wishes came to be established in the human society. The famous Psychologist Sigmund Freud has given the following opinion about the concept of almighty God :-

"Freud And Religion

Sigmund Freud (1856–1939) deals with the origins and nature of religious belief in several of his books and essays. Freud regards God as an illusion, based on the infantile need for a powerful father figure; religion, necessary to help us restrain violent impulses earlier in the development of civilization, can now be set aside in favor of reason and science.

In An Autobiographical Study, originally published in 1925, Freud recounts that "My parents were Jews, and I have remained a Jew myself." Familiarity with Bible stories, from an age even before he learned to read, had "an enduring effect on the direction of my interest." In 1873, upon attending the University at Vienna, he first encountered antisemitism: "I found that I was expected to feel myself inferior and an alien because I was a Jew."

In a prefatory note to the Hebrew translation of Totem and Taboo (1930) Freud describes himself as "an author who is ignorant of the language of holy writ, who is completely estranged from the religion of his fathers—as well as from every other religion" but who remains "in his essential nature a Jew and who has no desire to alter that nature".

In Obsessive Actions and Religious Practices (1907), his earliest writing about religion, Freud suggests that religion and neurosis are similar products of the human mind: neurosis, with its compulsive behavior, is "an individual religiosity", and religion, with its repetitive rituals, is a "universal obsessional neurosis."

The concept of an object of faith thus assured the people that they were not alone in their struggle for existence. They could take their recourse to such an omnipotent power in the hour of their need. This belief also drives out from the individuals the very best of their personal strength. The motivation provided by the religious faith adds to the inherent natural capability of the individuals.

✳ ✳ ✳

Appendix

Hindu Wisdom

The beauty of being a Hindu lies in your freedom to be who you want to be. Nobody can tell you what to do, or what not to do. There is no central authority, no single leader of the faith. No one can pass an order to excommunicate you, or like in some countries, pass a decree that orders your death by stoning for walking with a strange man.

We don't appreciate our freedom because we can't feel the plight of others who aren't free. Many religions have a central authority with awesome power over the individual. They have a clear chain of command, from the lowest local priest to the highest central leader. Hinduism somehow escaped from such central authority, and the Hindu has miraculously managed to hold on to his freedom through the ages. How did this happen? Vedanta is the answer. When the writers of Vedanta emerged, around 1500 BC, they faced an organized religion of orthodox Hinduism. This was the post Vedic age, where ritualism was practiced, and the masses had no choice but to follow. It was a coercive atmosphere.

The writers of Vedanta rebelled against this authority and moved away from society into forests. This was how the 'Aranyakas' were written, literally meaning 'writings from the forest'. These later paved the way for the Upanishads, and Vedanta eventually caught the imagination of the masses. It emerged triumphant, bearing with it the clear voice of personal freedom.

This democracy of religious thought, so intrinsic to Vedantic intelligence, sank into the mindset of every Indian. Most couldn't fathom the deep wisdom it contained, but this much was very clear. They understood that faith was an expression of personal freedom, and one could believe at will. That's why Hinduism saw an explosion of Gods. There was a God for every need and every creed. If you wanted to build your muscles, you

78

worshiped a God with fabulous muscles. If you wanted to pursue education, there was a Goddess of Learning. If it was wealth you were looking for, then you looked up to the Goddess of wealth — with gold coins coming out of her hands. If you wanted to live happily as a family, you worshiped Gods who especially blessed families. When you grew old and faced oncoming death, you spent time in contemplating a God whose business it was to dissolve everything — from an individual to the entire Universe.

Everywhere, divinity appeared in the manner and form you wanted it to appear, and when its use was over, you quietly discarded that form of divinity and looked at new forms of the divine that was currently of use to you. 'Yad Bhavam, tad Bhavati'... what you choose to believe becomes your personal truth, and freedom to believe is always more important than belief itself.

Behind all this — was the silent Vedantic wisdom that Gods are but figments of human imagination?

As the Kena Upanishad says, "Brahma ha devebhyo vijigye..." — All Gods are mere subjects of the Self. It implies that it is far better that God serves Man than Men serve God. Because Men never really serve God — they only obey the dictates of a religious head who speaks for that God, who can turn them into slaves in God's name.

Hindus have therefore never tried to convert anyone. Never waged war in the name of religion. The average Hindu happily makes Gods serve him as per his needs. He discards Gods when he has no use for them. And new Gods emerge all the time — in response to market needs. In this tumult, no central authority could survive. No single prophet could emerge and hold sway; no chain of command could be established.

Vedanta had injected an organized chaos into Hinduism, and that's the way it has been from the last thirty five centuries. Vedanta is also responsible, by default, for sustaining democracy. When the British left

India, it was assumed that the nation would soon break up. Nothing of that kind has happened. The pundits of doom forgot that the Indian had been used to religious freedom from thousands of years. When he got political freedom, he grabbed it naturally. After all, when you can discard Gods, why can't you discard leaders? Leaders like Gods are completely expendable to the Indian mindset. They are tolerated as long as they serve the people, and are replaced when needs change. It's the triumph of people over their leaders, and in this tumult, no dictator can ever take over and rule us. Strange! How the thoughts of a few men living in forests, thirty five centuries ago, can echo inside the heart of every Indian. That's a tribute to the resurgent power of India, and the fearlessness of its free thinking people.

✹ ✹ ✹